STUDYING THE OBOE

TECHNICAL EXERCISES AND STUDIES FOR OBOE
BY LIANG WANG

Order no. CH76945

Written by Liang Wang
Edited by Neil Pardoe
Cover design by Liz Barrand
Photo of Liang Wang by Matt Dine
Book design by Chloë Alexander
Music engraving by WR Music

With thanks to Ann Barkway,
Lizzie Moore and Uchenna Ngwe

Acknowledgements from the author
Special thanks to Dong Shu Yan, my Mother,
who taught me how to sing on the Oboe;
to Xiu De Wang, my Father, who always supported and loved what I did;
to Jing Guo Dong, my Uncle, who started the musical journey for me
and to Richard Woodhams, my dear teacher who will always be an inspiration in every way.

Printed in the EU

ISBN: 978-1-84938-568-8

CHESTER MUSIC
part of **WiseMusic**Group

EXCLUSIVELY DISTRIBUTED BY

HAL•LEONARD®

Visit Hal Leonard Online at
www.halleonard.com

Contact us:
Hal Leonard
7777 West Bluemound Road
Milwaukee, WI 53213
Email: info@halleonard.com

In Europe, contact:
Hal Leonard Europe Limited
42 Wigmore Street
Marylebone, London, W1U 2RY
Email: info@halleonardeurope.com

In Australia, contact:
Hal Leonard Australia Pty. Ltd.
4 Lentara Court
Cheltenham, Victoria, 3192 Australia
Email: info@halleonard.com.au

About the author

Liang Wang joined the New York Philharmonic in September 2006 as principal oboe. Previously, he was principal oboe of the Cincinnati Symphony Orchestra (2005–06), and principal oboe of the Santa Fe Opera in the 2004–05 season.

Born in Qing Dao, China, in 1980, Wang comes from a musical family. His mother was an amateur singer; his uncle was a professional oboist, and Wang began oboe studies with him at the age of seven. In 1993 he enrolled at the Beijing Central Conservatory, studying with Professor Zhu Dun, and two years later became a full-scholarship student at the Idyllwild Arts Academy in California. During his time there he was the Jack Smith Award Winner at the Pasadena Instrumental Competition, a two-time winner of the Los Angeles Philharmonic Fellowship, and a winner at the Spotlight Competition of the Los Angeles Philharmonic.

Wang completed his bachelor's degree in 2003 at the Curtis Institute of Music in Philadelphia, where he studied with the Philadelphia Orchestra's principal oboist Richard Woodhams. While at Curtis, he was a fellowship recipient at both the Aspen Music Festival and School, where he studied with John de Lancie, the former principal oboist of the Philadelphia Orchestra, and the Music Academy of the West, where he was a Career Grant recipient. Mr Wang was a prizewinner at the 2003 Fernard Gillet International Oboe Competition and a prizewinner at the 2002 Tilden Prize Competition.

Since graduating from Curtis, Wang has served as principal oboe with the San Francisco Ballet Orchestra, and as associate principal oboe of the San Francisco Symphony; he was also a guest principal oboist with the Chicago and San Francisco symphony orchestras. An active chamber musician, he has appeared at the Santa Fe Chamber Music Festival and the Angel Fire Music Festival. He has appeared as soloist with the San Francisco Ballet Orchestra in Richard Strauss's Oboe Concerto, and in Santa Fe, performing oboe concertos by Marcello and Vivaldi. He has given masterclasses at the Cincinnati Conservatory, was on the oboe faculty of the University of California at Berkeley, and is currently on the faculties of the Manhattan School of Music and New York University. Wang is also an honorary professor at the Beijing Central Conservatory.

Introduction

Dear friends,

Studying the Oboe is the perfect collection of exercises for oboists wanting to develop and refine their technique. The studies are suitable for all players of a good intermediate level and upwards. They range in length and standard from very basic exercises that make useful warm-ups for practice sessions, to longer, more challenging studies. They have been specifically written to develop and strengthen a variety of technical areas such as tone production, breath control, dynamic control, articulation and finger technique. They are presented in order of the keys covered – starting with sharp keys followed by flat keys. Tips are also included with many of the exercises to give students helpful hints and guidance with performance.

At the end of the exercises is an appendix of famous classical themes and orchestral excerpts which have been selected to offer students something a little more melodic to play after focusing on the technical aspects of the exercises. For each key used in the exercises there is a corresponding theme or excerpt, and in order to cover all these keys some themes have been transposed from their original orchestral versions.

Exercise 1

TIP Oboists are regularly required to play long As to enable other musicians to tune their instruments – therefore it's very important that you learn to produce a stable pitch on this note.

Exercise 2

Exercise 3

TIP Lift your 'G' finger as high as you can when you play from G to A in this exercise – it's one of your weakest fingers and this will help you to strengthen it. As you put the finger down make sure the movement is not too abrupt. You need to develop good control over this finger.

Exercise 4

Exercise 5

Exercise 6

TIP Think about passing the A as you play from G to B.

Exercise 7

TIP Make sure your two fingers move smoothly. A slur mark ⌒ means you should connect the notes without rearticulating.

Exercise 8

TIP This can be quite an unstable note due to the lack of holes covered, so you need to use your embouchure to control it. Position your mouth into the shape of an 'o', as if saying 'or'. This will help to flatten the pitch of the note and keep it more in tune.

Exercise 9

Exercise 10

Exercise 11

Exercise 12

Exercise 13

TIP This can be a difficult note to play at first because of the register. You need to use more air than for the previous notes. You don't need to blow too hard – just use more air as you would when singing in a low register.

Exercise 14

C major

Exercise 15

TIP It is very easy on the oboe to play a ⬦ on every note – however you should try to avoid doing this. Please listen to yourself carefully.

Exercise 16

 TIP Make sure you lift up your 4th and 5th fingers exactly together in order to get a smooth transition between C and E in this exercise.

Exercise 17

TIP In order to play the half hole for this note, you will need to roll the 1st finger of your left hand.

Exercise 18

Exercise 19

Exercise 20

Exercise 21

Exercise 22

Exercise 23

Exercise 24

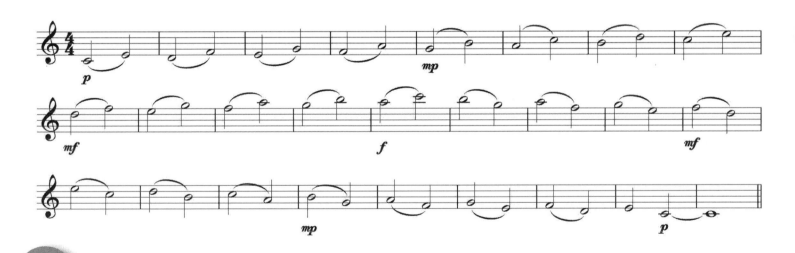

TIP   This is the first time dynamics are introduced. Make sure you observe them carefully.

- **Now try the Grand March theme on p.41**

Now try the Grand March theme on p.41

Exercise 25

A minor (harmonic)

Exercise 26

Exercise 27

TIP Make sure you play these two intervals very clearly – the articulation used makes this quite hard.
Try not to play them too harshly and aim for a warm and rich tone.

Exercise 28

• **Now try Polovtsian Dances theme on p.41**

Exercise 29

G major   Make sure this E does not stick out.

Exercise 30

Exercise 31

Exercise 32

TIP As with exercise 27, the articulation used here makes this quite hard.
Make sure the transition from C and B up to D is as smooth as possible.

Exercise 33

TIP Make sure the note values are carefully followed.

- **Now try Jesu, Joy Of Man's Desiring on p.42**

Exercise 34

E minor (harmonic)

Exercise 35

Exercise 36

Exercise 37

Exercise 38

Exercise 39

TIP Make sure the tongued and slurred notes are completely equal.

• **Now try the theme from Mozart's Symphony in G minor on p.42**

Exercise 40

D major

TIP Slurring from B to C♯ can be tricky – you need to make sure your fingers move simultaneously to achieve a smooth transition between the two notes.

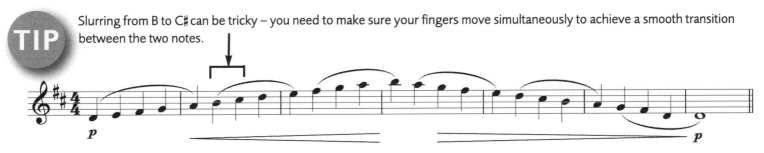

Exercise 41

Exercise 42

Exercise 43

TIP Make sure you practise this exercise slowly at first and then gradually build up your speed.

Exercise 44

• **Now try Minuet II on p.41**

Exercise 45

B minor

Exercise 46

• **Now try the theme from Swan Lake on p.43**

Exercise 47

A major

Exercise 48

Exercise 49

TIP Slurring between A and C can be tricky to play smoothly, check your hand motion in a mirror.

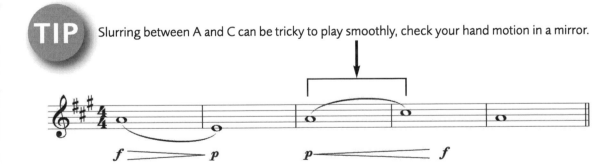

Exercise 50

Exercise 51

 When you play short and quick staccato notes like this, you need to keep the airflow through your oboe constant and use your tongue on the reed to start and stop the notes.

Exercise 52

- **Now try Ode To Joy on p.43**

Exercise 53

F♯ minor

Exercise 54

Exercise 55

Exercise 56

TIP Make sure the *crescendo* is gradual through to the last note, so that it doesn't suddenly stick out.

Exercise 57

TIP This is a fermata or 'pause' symbol ⌢, it means you should hold the note for longer than its value – how long is left to the player to decide.

• **Now try Fauré's Pavane on p.44**

Exercise 58

E major

Think of connecting the notes marked ⌢, even though you are rearticulating.

Exercise 59

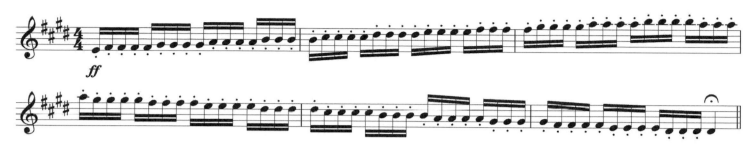

TIP Aim to keep the same quality of tone throughout this exercise. If you hear it diminishing, start again.

Exercise 60

Exercise 61

Exercise 62

Exercise 63

TIP Make sure you stay *pp* throughout this exercise.

• **Now try the theme from the Czech carol Rocking on p.43**

Exercise 64

C♯ minor

Exercise 65

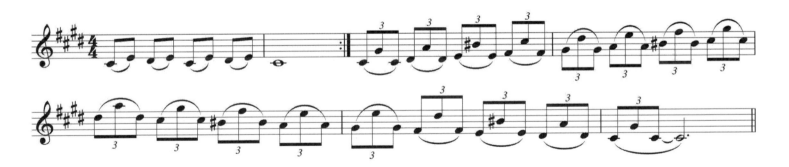

Exercise 66

Exercise 67

Exercise 68

TIP Make sure the last note does not stand out.

- **Now try the theme from Scheherzade on p.44**

Now try the theme from Scheherzade on p.44

Exercise 69

B major

Exercise 70

Exercise 71

TIPS

The low notes might be hard to articulate simply because of the register. Make sure you have a very relaxed embouchure as well as an open throat.

Playing a diminuendo down to low B is not easy – congratulate yourself once you achieve this!

Be careful not to play staccato notes too harshly – they should be short but also light.

• **Now try the theme from Jerusalem on p.45**

Here are the rest of the 'sharp' scales. You can apply any of the exercises to these scales.

Exercise 72

F♯ major

Exercise 73

D♯ minor

Exercise 74

C♯ minor

Exercise 75

A♯ minor

Exercise 76

F major

Exercise 77

Exercise 78

TIP Tongue the F as softly as you can.

Exercise 79

Exercise 80

• **Now try Danny Boy on p.45**

Exercise 81

D minor

Exercise 82

Exercise 83

TIP Going over the bridge between B♭ and C♯ is difficult. Pay close attention to your left hand and if you feel like you're losing control of the fingerings, practise the exercise slowly.

Exercise 84

Exercise 85

Exercise 86

Exercise 87

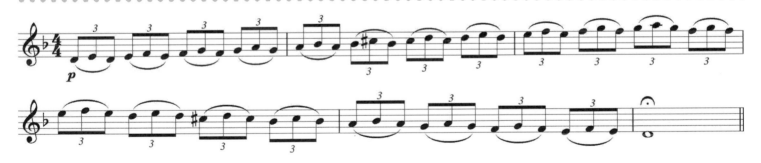

• **Now try Purcell's Rondeau theme on p.46**

Exercise 88

B♭ major

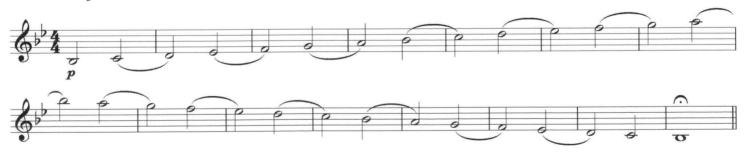

Exercise 89

Exercise 90

Exercise 91

TIP Remember not to ⟨⟩ during notes unless marked in the dynamics.

Exercise 92

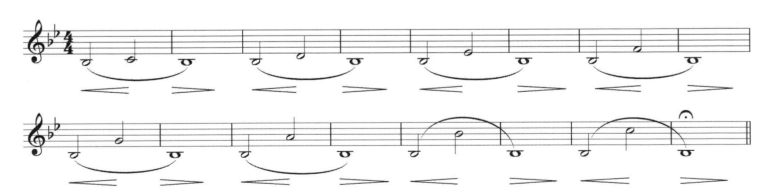

Exercise 93

Exercise 94

Exercise 95

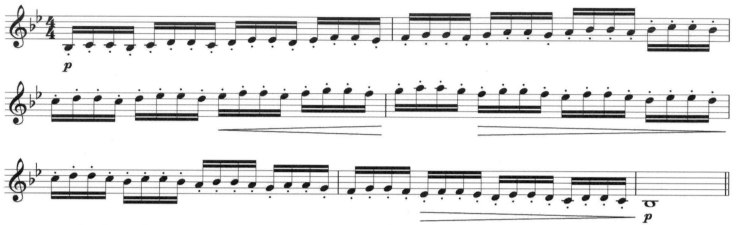

• **Now try the theme from March To The Scaffold on p.46**

Exercise 96

G minor

Exercise 97

Exercise 98

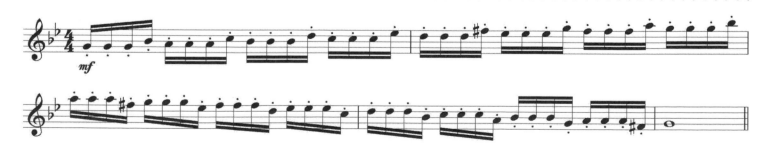

Exercise 99

molto legato

Exercise 100

TIP Lift the 3rd finger of your left hand as high as you can as you change from G to the higher notes – though only in this exercise!

Exercise 101

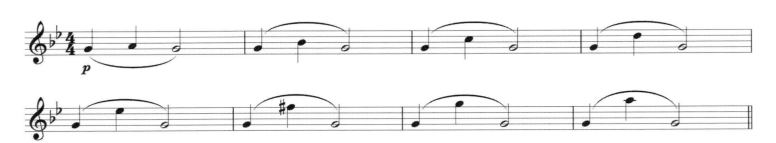

TIP Practise this very slowly! The purpose of this exercise is to make sure the intervals are properly sung.
Try to blend the slurred notes so that they're as smooth as you can possibly play them.

Exercise 102

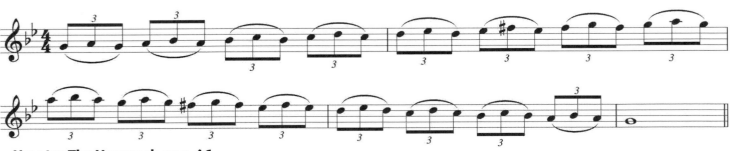

• **Now try The Hammock on p.46**

Exercise 103

E♭ major

Exercise 104

Exercise 105

TIP Make sure your airflow is continuous through the oboe, using only your tongue to start and stop the notes.
This is a great exercise for developing a warm and rich tone.

Exercise 106

Exercise 107

TIP Make sure you play through the phrase and keep the momentum going. Do not *crescendo* too early.

Exercise 108

Exercise 109

• **Now try 'Tis The Last Rose Of Summer on p.47**

Exercise 110

C minor

Exercise 111

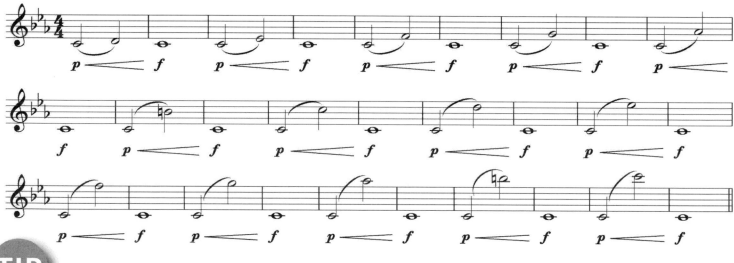

Exercise 112

TIP This exercise is to practise the connection between the notes!

Exercise 113

TIP Don't *diminuendo* too fast – make sure it is a gradual ————.

Exercise 114

TIP How expressively can you play this exercise?

Exercise 115

Exercise 116

Exercise 117

- **Now try the Prelude theme from L'Alésienne Suite No.1 on p.47**
Now try the Prelude theme from L'Alésienne Suite No.1 on p.47

Exercise 118

A♭ major

Exercise 119

Exercise 120

Exercise 121

Exercise 122

Exercise 123

Exercise 124

Exercise 125

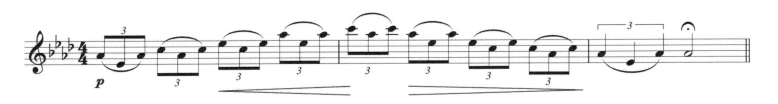

• **Now try the La Donna È Mobile theme from Rigoletto on p.47**

Exercise 126

F minor (harmonic)

Exercise 127

Exercise 128

Exercise 129

Exercise 130

Exercise 131

 TIP You will find this exercise much easier to play after exercise 130. The goal is to play a true legato, and playing exercise 130 first will help you to achieve this.

• **Now try the New World Symphony theme on p.48**

Exercise 132

D♭ major

Exercise 133

 TIP In this exercise it's very important not to play the low D♭ too flat.

Exercise 134

Exercise 135

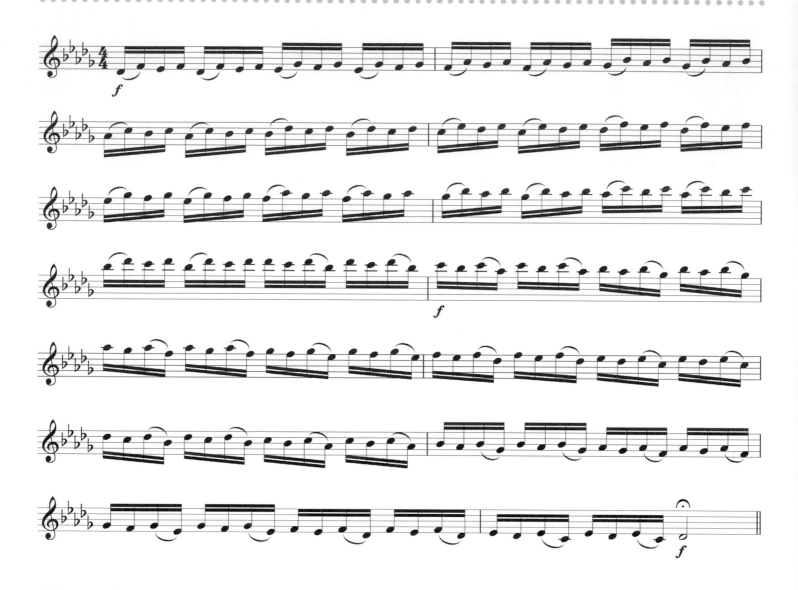

Exercise 136

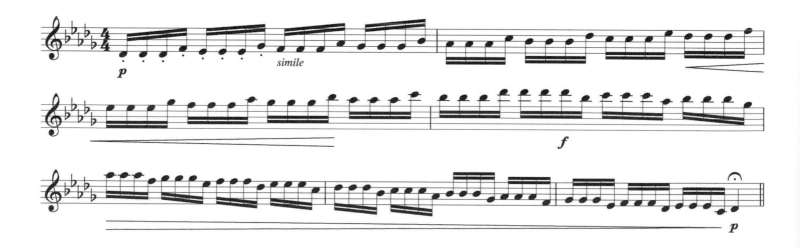

Exercise 137

Exercise 138

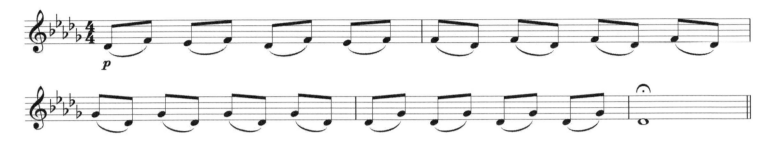

• **Now try the Non Più Andrai theme from The Marriage of Figaro on p.48**

Now try the Non Più Andrai theme from The Marriage of Figaro on p.48

Exercise 139

B minor (harmonic)

Exercise 140

Exercise 141

Exercise 142

Exercise 143

Exercise 144

Exercise 145

Exercise 146

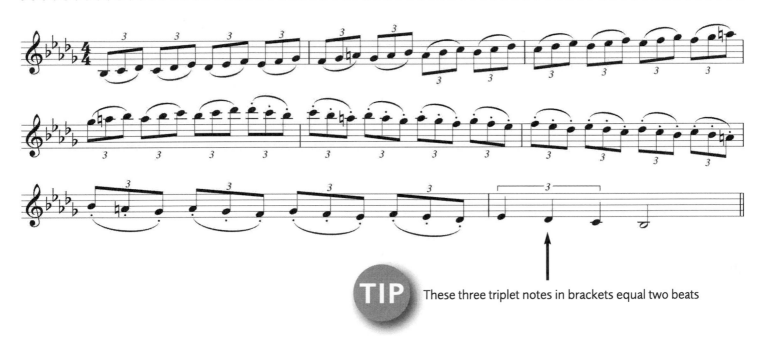

TIP These three triplet notes in brackets equal two beats

- **Now try the theme from Tchaikovsky's Symphony No.4 on p.48**

Here are the rest of the 'flat' scales. Apply any of the previous exercises to these scales.

Exercise 147

G♭ major

Exercise 148

E♭ minor (harmonic)

Exercise 149

C♭ major

Exercise 150

A♭ minor (harmonic)

Themes & Excerpts

Grand March theme from *Aida*

Verdi

With breadth

Polovtsian Dances theme from *Prince Igor*

Borodin

Andantino

p con espress. e dolce

Minuet II from *Music for the Royal Fireworks*

Handel

Allegro

Jesu, Joy Of Man's Desiring

J.S. Bach

With easy movement

Theme from Symphony in G minor (1st movement) K.550

Mozart

With movement

Theme from *Swan Lake*

Tchaikovsky

Ode To Joy theme from Symphony No.9 (last movement)

Beethoven

Rocking

Traditional Czech Carol

Pavane

Fauré

Theme from *Scheherazade* (2nd movement)

Rimsky-Korsakov

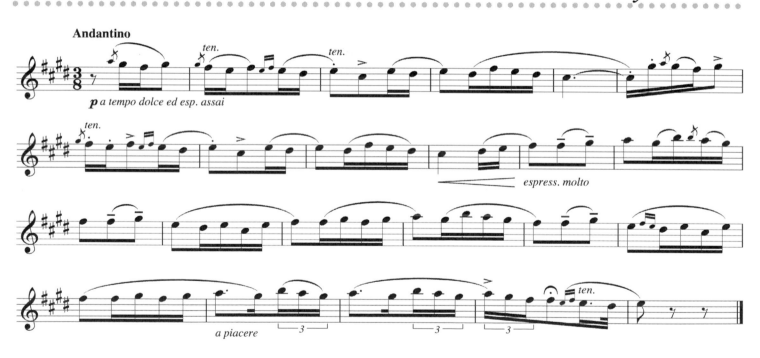

Theme from *Jerusalem*

Parry

Danny Boy

Traditional Irish

Rondeau theme from *Abdelazar*

Purcell

March To The Scaffold theme from *Symphony Fantastique*

Berlioz

The Hammock

Traditional Mexican

'Tis The Last Rose of Summer

Traditional Irish

Prelude theme from *L'Arlésienne Suite No.1*

Bizet

La Donna È Mobile theme from *Rigoletto*

Verdi

Theme from Symphony No.9 (4th movement)

Dvořák

Allegro con fuoco

Non Più Andrai theme from *The Marriage of Figaro*

Mozart

Vivace

Theme from Symphony No.4 (2nd movement)

Tchaikovsky

Andantino in modo di canzona

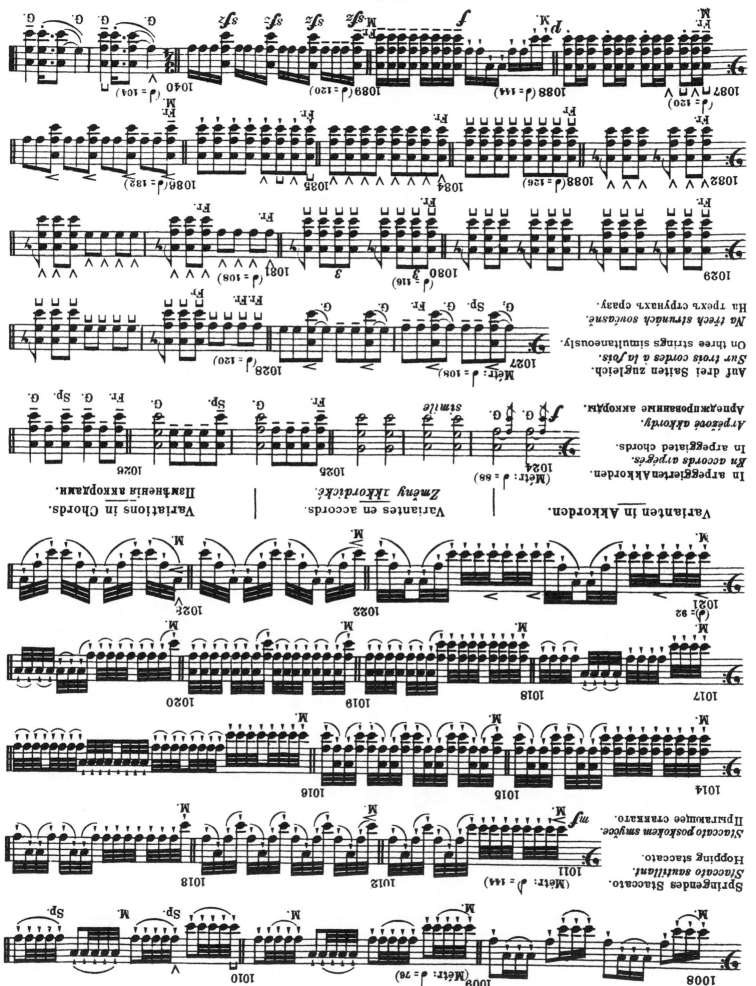